NEW CHATTO [illegible]

NUMBER TWO

NEW CHATTO POETS
NUMBER TWO

SUSANNE EHRHARDT

PAUL MAY

LUCY ANNE WATT

ROBERT CRAWFORD

SARAH MAGUIRE

MARK FORD

For all at Villiers Park,
with best wishes,

Sarah Maguire

13. X. 89.

Chatto & Windus
LONDON

Published in 1989 by
Chatto & Windus Ltd
30 Bedford Square
London WC1B 3SG

A CIP Catalogue record for this book is available
from the British Library

ISBN 0 7011 3393 7

Photoset by Rowland Phototypesetting Ltd
Bury St Edmunds, Suffolk
Printed in Great Britain by
Redwood Burn Ltd
Trowbridge, Wiltshire

CONTENTS

MARK FORD

NEW CHATTO POETS NUMBER TWO

SUSANNE EHRHARDT

Chor Chandia

for Zafrullah

In late May 1985 a tidal bore struck the south-eastern coast of Bangladesh, causing widespread devastation and loss of life.

1

Either side of the bund nobody slept
That night. It wasn't the siren warning
(The third time this year), but the wind's cling
And the way frisky things stayed wrapped
About uprights, legs or gateposts, till swept
By a sidling gust up and away, a strange falling
Towards the sky. Later, the wind was king
And all things frisky; roofs like sheets danced rapt
To his bidding, the living bowed over earth lapped
By early tongues of the tide gathering
At sea. Freak moon joined freak wind to fling
Water on water, a phantom mountain capped
With snowy froth. Rearing, Jaganath leapt
For the bund across the new lands levelling
All. But of this we on the safe side know nothing,
Their deaths, like their America, unmapped.

2

On the whole, earth is a slow process,
An accretion of slight forces, singly trivial;
Eruptions cool and harden through ages,
Frost breaks, water whittles,
Change without becoming, always provisional.

Earth's age is reckoned in years.
Medieval man taught a few thousand, assumed
Human need conjured her from the mind of God.
Science adds noughts, makes us modest;
We talk of geological and human time.
Contemplating the scooping of a nook in a cave
Resembles the contemplation of eternity.

But in the Bay of Bengal earth, whale-like,
Humps from the sea, barely tumescent, dimly defined,
Grows green in a matter of seasons
And extends her ambiguous welcome
To herds, ploughs, homesteads, our kind of life.

3
Wind blew salt and sun,
Blackened our skin, carved wrinkles;
But its steady tug busied us
Tucking, fixing, fetching, weighing down,
Kept our eyes to the ground
When looking up, there was nothing
For them to alight on in the vast
Flowing with the sky.

No height except our own,
No corner, edge, outline,
Nothing but blurred gradations
Of low and lower still,
Land-green, water-brown, sky-grey,
Amphibious, indeterminate;
Not yet land
But the raw material only.

That was before we came.
We, eyes level and garments kilted,
Dug soil from the tide-bound,
Basket by basketful raised
Islands of constant dryness.
We drove home stakes to corner
Our houses, squared bamboo,
Angled our roofs with precision.

We planted, the fast-growing first,
And rejoiced when the banana
Stood taller than we.
In time, palms will rise,
Signs of us against the sky.
The vast no longer clings so closely,
But distant packs of pie dogs
Weep nightly for the moon.

4
The bore left such flotsam
That for days only children
Ventured across the bund, children
Grieving for their sheep. They saw,
Where the green land had donned
Such a sudden dun blossoming,
Among clumps of fleeces, stilled
But for the ruffling of the wind,
The grievous sight
Of their own kind sprawled in death.
And having seen one, their eyes,
Grown in the way of it, picked out more.
They wandered on, calling to each other
The tally, as children elsewhere

May call through summer woods
Their troves of berries and mushrooms,
Voices stranged by space.
For the rest, the dead were alone
Under the fierce sun wheeling in the sky.
Six-hourly, the tide's flow
Lifted them slowly, cradled them softly,
Six-hourly, they drifted aground with the ebb.

5
It started to rain when they came,
Through mud and shallows, at the end
Of a long day of burying to bury her
Who had lain there too long.

Driving rain cut them adrift in a world
Of grey, stung their burnt skin as they
Stood shivering, sounded a plangent drum
On the bloated belly of her cow.

Her cow? Or someone else's? How far
Had she travelled the Bay, dipping and bobbing,
Before fetching up on this knoll of grass?
Was it she bore the children they buried?

From the matted tangle still holding her skull
And her single plastic bracelet they knew her
A woman, and poor. The manner of her death
Spoke her courage. Perhaps it was enough.

They cut a shallow grave, for the earth
Was heavy and their arms ached.
Sodden straw washed up against her hid
The white flux heaving between her legs.

Lifting her with care, she was so friable,
They found her breasts grown earthlike,
Scuttling with life as the underside
Of a stone slab levered from dankness.

They held their breath for the sick-sweet
Smell of her passing as she slid awkwardly
Into her grave, and crumbled earth,
Murmuring prayers for her immortal soul.

6
Envoi
A small mirror in
The swath of debris
Where she had been,

Framed in embroidery
Of coloured thread
From an old sari.

A hand, a head,
An eye for beauty
Made it.

I've worked it out

I've worked it out that when my parents parted
some time at the end of '43
I was about the size of a pea
eroding the lining of mum's womb.
He had been on compassionate leave
for grandfather's terminal illness, hence,
amid the stink of death that was Europe,
their chance to make life.

I know it like a memory, the walk to the station
with their arms hooked (that's how couples
walked those days), he in Luftwaffe uniform,
blue-grey, her favourite colour always,
she in the coat with the fox fur collar.
They talked of how it would be when it was over.
She saw the train out and walked back,
spent the rest of the pregnancy ducking bombs,
watching the city subside into rubble.

There was no news, but the letters stopped,
so he was listed missing. Someone claimed
to have seen him in Estonia, five hundred miles
from where he was last known to be.
She went to the fortune-teller who said
he'd be back in '51, or if not, by '53.
Later, she had him declared dead
for the sake of the war widow's pension.
All that time, I spooned the hated potato soup –
one for mummy, one for sister, one for granny,
three for father starving in the camp.

In '55, Adenauer negotiated the release
of the last POW's in Soviet hands.
Aged eleven, I watched her watch the trains go by.
Leaning from open wagons other men waved to us,
excited so soon after crossing the border.
It was then she gave up and wept.

Footnotes to the Tour Report

1. Flying in

Nothing but the curl of my toes keeps this thing
Airborne, or it would slip to meet its wispy shadow
Edging below across deserted villages, encroaching desert.
How long is a piece of string? Or a cat's life?
I must put my affairs in order before the next haul.
The pilot selects auto, sits back and lights a cigarette.
Exhausted, I fall asleep, and sleeping, fall.

2. On the face of it

Shops shuttered, few about, bursts of birdsong obtrude
In muted streets. On the face of it a starving town
Looks like an English Sunday. I had to be told
That this was not rest but running down. Then I saw
The absences, of youngest and oldest, of those
Who stayed by quenched cooking-fires, of those
Who walked from the wasted countryside in hope of food,
And finding none, turned back, thinner for the exercise.

3. Buying grain

There is still a little trading. On the pavement
Someone set up with his bag of grain. A customer
Examines a scoop, discards a stone,
Lets it patter through her hand, still as rain.
To pay that price she must have sold a treasure.
She spreads her cloth. A hole needs staunching
With a rag. He measures carefully and pours.
It worries me, what if that rag rucks and grain

Spills on the journey home? Could she not borrow
Something whole when each spilt handful
Might have bought an hour's life? Perhaps she'd say
That, anyway, so little food is little more than none.

4. Hooch

The French mechanic's local wife is a dab hand
At the distillery. She shows me her apparatus
And how it's done: well-water drawn with muddy rope,
Dates (the last consignment from the North
Till who knows when), for strength and sweetness.
Gravely, we sit on gravelled space inside the fence
And sip. It's good, smooth and slippery to the throat.
They reckon cycling to the border when it gets bad
Will take three days or so, living off the bush.
We'll get out tomorrow. We walk back through patches
Of yellow-flowering groundnut, fields of young maize,
Hiding the bottle, hiding our laughter,
Ambling demurely past the police.

5. Strategic Meeting

We meet to discuss possibilities, relative advantages
Of river and road, how long it takes from here to there,
How many bridges need repair, which roads are mined,
Which safe from bandits or guerrilla bands, fordability
Of rivers swollen by recent rains. We go on to tonnages
And petrol consumption, insurance, drivers' wages.
Meanwhile, perhaps an airlift, for speed?
But one would need three Hercules a day to feed
The population of the town, not to speak of those
Who would come from the countryside once the news

Got round, and the strip wouldn't take it. In any case,
Without a ceasefire, the whole thing is moonshine.
We talk and talk, break up to beat the curfew.

6. Tomorrow

We sit on packed bags, grounded by rain.
Across the empty compound they shelter
Under streaming eaves with no bags to pack.
Our time and theirs runs off the glistening
Laterite outcrops, thickens in red-brown puddles.
We wait to go, back to our lives, our loves,
Our hard houses.

In the South

Driving north all day,
Deeper than can be done gently,
The engine and the rush of air
In our faces spare us the sounds
Which shoals of panicked goats might make,
Or men, thrashing confused cattle off the verge,
Or women, crucified to their wide loads,
Straightening painfully and veering
For us to pass – a foreign body
Driving into the flesh of the place.

The ancient work of rivers –
Gorges, plateaus, escarpments tripping
Down and down toward the rangeland haze;
The recent work of men – stone houses,
Sloping fields: every bend in the road
Cancels the images, refurnishes the retina

Until edges blunt, colours blend.
But he, drinking from the roadside trickle,
Folded up flatter than man was meant to fold,
Sees us as a passing blur.

We stop for a piss. Sudden quiet
Emits a solitary trill, sweats flybuzz.
Stiff from sitting still, I pick for cover
Through ripe sorghum clattering like bones.
The sibilant stream splashes on hard earth,
Chases an iridescent beetle, seeps
With a faint click, darkening the ground.
And after our waking, to sound and smell,
To being scratched, stung, seen,
We climb into the dream again, relieved.

Song

She did for me with the first pluck
on her strung gourd spilling outward
like rings of water and the long wail
leading into her song of Krishna
and kingfishers, of how to ride
the crest of the wave without drowning.
She was all toothless gums
stained with pan juice, her throat a cave.
People said, when she needed firewood
she made the tree in her yard drop a branch.
I shouted for encores like a drunk,
emptied my purse in her lap. She cackled,
raking it in, 'I did tell God this morning
to give me something.'

Abstracting medical papers

In a study conducted in Leningrad, the effects of adjuvant chemotherapy on 1228 breast cancer patients was compared to the effect of mastectomy only . . .

Bath, bedroom mirror, lover's caress –
To each her own annunciation, to each
Her disbelief. Not I; if I, not yet.

From now on, a hand near the switch –
At night, squares of light chequer
The housing estates. Who walked much

Watching the Neva drift ice, pack and stir
Again in due season are walking still,
Strain to reason with their fickle future;

Grow tired. The anaesthetist's needle,
The surgeon's knife exact their fiat –
What more did Mary do? – Waking, they will

Mourn their symmetry. By the poison cabinet,
Gloved, gowned and goggled, a stranger draws
The stuff to chase the spill. The lancet

Punctures more than skin – It prickles
Up my arm, I taste it in my mouth – Yes,
The taste of life now, such as it is.

Oath of Allegiance

I swear by Almighty God that

Not knowing the local spirits and how to appease them
She became a watcher, developed a feel for things so acute
It was almost fey. She moved with care. At their rituals
She hung herself about with smiles when her tongue sought,
But did not quite succeed, to form the incantations.
Rarely quite right, and without the right to be rude,
She found being nice the safest way to be.

On becoming a British citizen

Behind her, the burnt-out house, walls peeling because
They whitewashed over the wet – life must go on.
They had struck a bargain by scrabbling and skimping
And minding their words in front of the children,
So that the edges of fields did not commemorate corpses,
Or the shunting-yard inadmissible freight. In the end,
It was to be gone that she went, not to become.

I will be faithful and bear true allegiance

The Book in one hand she stands to intone the spells
Which *we* her *they* and wonders how. Take, for instance,
The space in her mind the shape of a stag-beetle's
  mandible,
A smooth, veined pebble has filled it. The difference
Proved smaller than at first appeared – both objects shout,
Look what I found. But such swaps show up a valence
Or a looseness perhaps tending to betrayal.

To Her Majesty Queen Elizabeth the Second Her Heirs and Successors

And it's not a straight swap either, but more like crossing
A river – where you fetch up depends, among other factors,
On how long it took. Given time and a current,
The landing place will lie downstream as much as across,
Even though the drift eludes eyes scanning the other bank.
In this office in this town she stands and wonders
How far she has gone from where she saw herself go.

According to law

After all, it is a mere formality, but stately formulae
Have a way of tricking into a spurious awe.
To cover up they fuss with signatures and stamp-pad.
We're good at oaths, he jokes, hints at the local disco.
She pleads unsocial working-hours and her age. He, crisply,
That will be three pounds then (the statutory fee slow
To catch up with inflation). It's a bargain, at the price.

PAUL MAY

Dating

The beer garden is an earth pit
Behind a theatre. It was to be
A community resource centre
But the money dried up.
I read it in the *Mercury*.
In the unhappy hour
Predictable people from all walks
Gather there to forge new links
And other currencies.

The speakers relay the shipping forecast
But everyone talks of
How time is money
And money time.
A nation of shopkeepers
In dry-dock, being refitted.

Maurice is a dignified minority
No art historian he
No casual bumboy
Not one to mince his words.
He gets chatting to a videogrocer
(Something in the raincoat business)
And between them
Condensed failure drips
From the tarpaulin awning.

I am in the kitchen
Reading labels.

Helpful men have warned me
When the milk will wear out.
I shall chalk a similar date
One day outside the beer garden.
For the mad hatter
Knew he would die
On the tenth of the sixth.

Animal magnet

The wet nurses, blowzy in the wind,
Fell in line on the cliff path.

In the days when I was eclipsed,
Septimus took a dark bite out of me.
He sweated in a cloth nailed to a wall,
He squalled in his imitation of cats,
And his drool was molten silver spoons.

Dank and shifty, I went to pay my slow respects
To the sea, lying amber like a dish of piss.
Flies swimming in a blocked drain.
I threw branches from the edge
But could not make
The water pull itself back.
The lodestone was elsewhere in its influential circles.

Mother sniggering into someone's beer,
Then mopping up the splashes with soda bread,
While the boy slept easy,
Inheriting the earth from under my feet.

She had trained me for my business
By rubbing my face in it
When I did it.

I learned all the right responses,
But Septimus never got so far,
Like his brothers and sisters,
All piled up in the hillside.
She made cheese again that winter
And sold it from a basket by the road.

There was more tin as a result.
I remember the Northern Lights,
Pastel sheets warping on the air,
Mother stirring over a low heat.

Furniture Green

I

This is me at the last opening,
Famous types in tow.
This is me on a self-made corner,
Offering models in sticks and stones.
This is me in sixty-three,
Throwing my step-shadow round a corner.

I am the spoilt son
Running to seed under a low bridge,

Stuck fuck up against the brickwork
With neither moat nor mortgage,
Lock stock nor barrel.

I walk under the biggest ladder.
A train goes over my head
Like a strip of old film.

2
They chose Blue Murder for my room,
It's all very restful, I don't think.

I thought I had an empty day
But there are people pencilled in.

I send them through at intervals
And imagine they leave by other doors.

They wear 405-line suits
And drop their thumbprints on a table.

They think to pass their habits on to me.
I could be all mirror in a fitting room.

I, said Sparrow, with my Eton and Harrow,
I gave this woman away.

I wrap up against the cold
In a quiet five-pound note.

3
Orange is all over a wrong sky
And the bride is the tail
Of a catherine wheel.

A child leans over the edge
Of a long weekend.

The windows could be in the hills
And the shrunken animals
Walking round the groom's hat-brim.

I see all the hands in his pockets,
And all the stars prickling through
The floorboards or ploughed fields.

The food remains uneaten
And the man from the next town
Holds a glass plate and a blackout.

4
She was like something dug up,
Paler than almond or garlic.

The snow grew blond on its way from the east
And turned us into souvenirs.

At all times we were the wooden couple
Who live in the clock and think

Of nothing but weather.
Then I was landlocked.

Sometimes I want to lie back
And pull a white line around me.

But I marvel at the square they've made,
Neat as handkerchief,

And the family drops hand over hand
From my open wallet.

Harvests

Dolly missed the wars,
The speeches in the big barn.
She knew that the boys had left
And been replaced each October
By young men from the city
Who came to howk the tattie trenches.

Other women took them in,
Scrubbed their skins
And carved out their eyes.
The broken horse took advantage,
Stamped like a senator,
Stood and gassed in the wintering fields.

She joined the other women on the shore
And saw the stars and moon
Beaten like steel into the surface of the sea,
And the men on the sand
Stumble up to the treasury
With their shell chests.

GI Brides

Daisy, Violet, Rose,
Washing day below deck,
Girls and linen in public.

Evening falls behind them,
With the pebbles falling in London,
The crumbs everywhere.

With little room in the ship,
It takes two to fold a letter.

The ship lives in celluloid
Which curls at the furthest end,
The rim of America,

Where upholstered men
Wait in twelve o'clock shadows,
For Daisy, Violet, Rose.

By the Embankment

There was demolition
Spot on a certain hour
When we landed in the street
And the pubs came down like dominoes.

We men would meet in the sooty field,
Pose in the stubble and toast ourselves.
It was a good crack, real exclusive;
Until I swelled out of fashion.

(By the Embankment
Women catch my pudding and pie
And run so slowly, like the river.)

That night I got the message, separated myself
And toured the beds of broken green glass.
Eminent men had fallen asleep
Under eyeshades and gin bottles;
And we were only saving places.

The English know how to queue,
They have a patience which forgets ends,
They don't really want to arrive.
I could learn to manage
And to measure a prospect.
I could go along with that,
Fall in with this.

I've been all around the houses
Like a long piece of dark water,
My eyes down for coins.

Eliza smiles

She prayed to her sirens, simple ocean pearls,
When she undressed. It was another tongue.

Young Sir picked her up on her manners
And blew hot and cold. He found fault

And stuffed it with Brummagem;
It's the only language you people understand.

She wished for the travelling fair
Where she'd sparkled for the great man:

The Lovely, the Delightful . . .
They drank her, something wicked.

Gas flowers from the wall each four o'clock
When Eliza smiles and comes to knock.

Master doesn't know she exists. She appears
With a bright tray, laden with a memory game.

Aquation

Marriage, the civil engine,
Jump-starts behind headstones;
Amidst the broken faces of angels
And the periscopes . . .

His family finds its level
In the brimming cemetery,
Solved and dissolved
Like bits of plankton algebra.

He recalls
Whispering bitter nothings
To the backless little number
That became identity;
Rehears compromises
Telescoping in crowds
Of couples concatenating . . .

Marriage, essential prop,
Does all the voices:
Siren, thunder,
The call to the country.

He spends half his time
Feeding the machine and half
Appalled at its momentum.
He digs his garden
And dreams displacement:

His exact weight in water
Falling as rain

Relays

Her father was unforgettable.
He was in all the columns,
Was always running through,
Fleeting, never for long in evidence.

He was washed onto everything
While I stuck at nothing,
This was the idea.

In my days lost to the nation
I left my shrug on the back of the door.

She comes away with nothing,
Shedding plaster and next door behind her,
Everywhere she's been and what got broken there.

I climb down all day
And I'm not the man I had in mind,
Who walked across the flat roofs
In summer and carried a doorway
For autumn, a torch for winter.

Walter and Connie

They walk back after the boat-burning,
Arm in arm like loose paper chain.
They will see themselves in the pictures.
They have queued outside every Gaumont
And seen the world in cinemascope,
In the bowl of a spoon.

Connie's dream house is laminated,
Town-gassed. A saucer by the bed
For Walter's change and key.

Still flames hang under the tide,
Practise in the mirror.

Walter carries Connie
Across an unseen line
And comes to her like echo.

Periodicity

This particular sauceboat,
He gets none.

My aunt finishes sewing up
My mother's legs, so she can go out
To the war looking her best.
I'm not allowed any of the
Peculiarly tipsy trifle,
Because I've spoken out of turn.
Or been in the knifebox again.
I still want to know why
My mother says she's got the painters in,
When we're still surrounded by
The same old tangle of flat flowers . . .

My father came in from the war
And showed me *his* decoration:
For the repetition of a small design.

I think now of the bloody utility fleet,
Small town England all at sea,
And a lighthouse breaking up rocks;

Evasion expected daily.

The partition of the opera

There was a secret word
At the stage-door.
So I hid in a bunch of flowers.
I went step after step.

The building was veined
With ropes and infested
With spectacled men,
Spatter-dressed men with press cards.
It was auction.
All call and response.
I crept behind cottons and silks,
I made like a coathanger.
I saw the breathing on,
And the great man slip away
And sit the same.
And there was luggage blooming
From the air, and train tickets,
And they had words.
Oh I was fit to shrivel up
Crawl into a hole in the ground.
They flashed her from all angles
On her splendid exit.
She went to emulsion,
To crystals, and to a thousand dots.

Burrbond

A handkerchief full of houses
Over one shoulder, Burrbond
Pauses and wipes his crown.
Lands fall about
And the river dips and preens
Like signature.
He sets up shop
Borrowing a sign for the present.

They all come to gape at Burrbond,
Intent with spade
Mixing sugar and water windows.
Behind him behind him
Property takes shape.
It appreciates like nothing on earth.
Forward parties flutter down
And lodge behind the sashes.

They pitch and toss,
Crapping stucco. Burrbond
Walks under the bunting,
Exercising his options
In the sudden street.
He has designs on the distance.
He scratches a cloud
And the ground blisters.

LUCY ANNE WATT

The camp

Fresh as yesterday, the smell of the bay-hedge,
and dust, through our Daimler's windows;
the drive curving so unctuously
I thought that, too, wished for this marriage.

We stopped. And there were the two attendants,
stepping calmly, their faces bright,
a ballet of pale knee, Blanco-ed toe,
and something – I couldn't quite see – uniting their hands.

I panicked – a little. But I wasn't silly.
They took me firmly by the elbows,
and I didn't resist. Ten shallow steps.
I thought: this is exactly how it should be.

And the Groom in the vestry waiting,
in a thin, truncated coat, the solemn
unembroidered bands drifting from his lapels
to the strange brass flower I call Oedema's Fob.

I saw him. He moved towards me. It seemed
all shadows drew in. My heart fluttered,
for a little while, sang. Their hands,
their voices all gentle, focused, kind.

(The method, I learned much later, is conventional.
Soft pressure on the arm.
Flowers in the room. A white, transparent nightie,
against which, all doors stayed locked.

And they tease with terms. they refer,
tenderly, to rest, and strength, and loving care.
The soul, it seems, is weighed on bathroom scales.
They admire my wrists and ankles. Examine

my fluids for their sins. And if I speak
– naturally – of when, and how, and who –
they soothe with careful humour; or illicit sips
of Sacred Wine, and tiny pale-pink sweets;

or spiritedly, take my arms, and fold them
one across the other, so that, as if in practice,
I hug myself
in fold on fold of damp, limp sheet.

Sometimes, I sit with the Confessor,
who reads, and notes, from an Open Testament
inscribed with my full name, dates,
and the names of those others, who gave me away.)

After a day or two, I suspected the hard new bed.
And the breakfast tray, with letters and lilies.
The women with hairbrushes, identical smiles.
The too-short visits of my unnervous Groom.

But I was patient, walking the garden, smelling bay,
feeling myself preserved, fresh, unused,
perfect, against my Husband's belated visit.
And when he came – when he did – how the door would
burst its hinges,

all doors would loosen, and the waiting unimpatient guests,
the faces, emergent in the corridor,
the shy, shifting strangers, who treasure biscuits,
and sing, covertly, hankies at mouth.

– all these would stride from bed, toilet, fire-escape,
clinking glasses; all these, shedding winceyette,
and dull frilled nylon, and supernumerary teeth,
would mesh their limbs, and groins, and quilts,

and us, in one long night of unsolemn consummation.
Patience, I said, in view of this. Patience. But it was hard,
The Groom's face continually changing,
the attendants swapping features, hair.

(But to kill time, I've imagined I'm writing a novel.
It's about a Camp. A small knot of squalid huts
squeezed by frozen wastes,
and the shadow of a huge, semi-derelict, Terminal
  Hospital.

Here (the heroine) I am banished
for a term of not less than seven hard years
after an interesting, internationally famous trail,
watched keenly (among others) by the Revolutionary
  Press.

Oh, and despite my pallor,
trembling lips, and prematurely sunken cheeks
– I love it all. The notoriety. Public scuffles.
Hands straining, like wind, to brush my scudding coat.

the wind itself booming with éclat. To acknowledge which
I give, at the prison van, a last, mournful wave,
breaking, in its course, and subsequent photographic
  reproduction,
ten hundred score of hearts.

And the satisfaction then – to be about to die for ideology!
Or perhaps to suffer just up to the point
where one's not quite allowed . . .?
Whichever way, privation (as I should know) ennobles
  beauty,

kindling heart from thin, sucked skin, and probing bones.
It's an easy trick – to make the eyes
enlarge and burn. I used to practise once.
But they heaped my plate. Admonished.)

So, planning the above, as a new, then less new bride,
time passed. It passed at a different rate
after a bit. I clung, stubbornly, to prison fiction,
peculiar syntax of walls and rules,

terminology which, otherwise, I'd lack.
And though it's secret, I drew it once,
for the persuasive woman who peddles clay, and paint.
I drew (without equivocation) a sort of thick dark glass
  vessel,

with walls too slippery to climb, and one door only,
labelled from 'out' to 'in'. This is where
the Confessor comes, and I can't pass.
But in the middle, I didn't know what to put:

as what is, really, unmetaphorically, inside?
My brush hovered, then. Finally, I chose a rack,
which was supposed to demonstrate
the psychological inferiority of the Camp.

Because, as I explained, carefully, to the Pedlar,
flesh hurts in a different way from the spirit,
and may recover, knowing that, by convention,
protest is noble; and only the ignominious

suffer, without choice. And when
she frowned, I said that, actually,
no one would compete with the original pain;
the birth-right's original horror, and trap.

She smiled. I think she admired the painting,
if she didn't understand. Anyway, we bartered:
that, for a hank of wool, from which
I've knitted, so far, socks, and a blue balaclava.

But all brides must be equally submissive, and polished,
and fill their time. For instance,
on Wednesdays I mend my lingerie;
on Fridays, knit; on Mondays, confess, and pray.

The Groom, meanwhile, grows a dapper moustache.
An attendant expects. Though the visitors
fell off, one by one, over the course of three
exceptionally hard, long winters.

By the way, a bride should also know Socrates
and keep a little hemlock in her trunk. That,
together with a diaphragm, and a strictly observed routine,
is, I think, essential.

Of funerals

Staying with Auntie Annie and Uncle Jack,
we paid for hot baps with a silver threepence –
so thin you could slide it between your teeth.

Life, for a Scotsman, was always a matter of costing up.
We thought of you, all through the service,
eager to economise, but anxious to do what's fit.

We had the plainest coffin, then, but were frivolous
with the flowers, and quibbled over the price
of the funeral meats. 'Lead us, Heavenly Father, lead
us . . .'

There should have been a piper. We should have
taken you back north, in the steps of Grandma Flora,
in the guard's van, in her oak.

You'd paid a sixpence for the porter, a florin for the cab,
and Flora, the £2.4s.9d.
for the plot in a secondary cemetery

where you laid her with your dad.
She wore a rakish felt, stripped of ribbon, flower.
And Mama, a turquoise suit, to follow in your wake.

All through that final day, familiar, comic stress,
matching want to expectation; fiddling measure, weight;
and fluttery, creative counting of mourners, messages,
bouquets.

Though nothing blots the way we lost the coffin,
the waste of fine wood, brass and bones;
and the shadow of the crematorium on wreaths,

extravagant, with bows. 'When you're ready. But . . .'
The undertaker shifted, indicating further press
of burial and burn. And payment would come later –

slick transfer from the estate; no truck with silver,
brass, rendre compte; argument you liked.
And then, a tip. But I saw you in the bushes,

frowning, jiggling your loose change,
as our car kicked up the gravel,
gates opened; losers, we got away to . . .

the homecoming, disappointment, guests.
After, another drop, tidying round your photographs,
wondering what to do, and how they'd know

which ashes were really, truly you. Well,
whatever turned up later in a screw-top, plastic urn,
we ferried to the Pentlands, spread our hands, and watched
them go.

Open-cast mining

Sometimes, a band would come back singing
through the lane's dust, hands solicitous
with prizes: shy aconites, rich fan of leaves,
some half-cupped nest, a blue, scoured shell.

Beeches straddled the rise. Chalk's slippery
scree knifed shadows cool as pools.
Sunning, girls feathered pallor with lemon.
The boys, deeper in, pared sticks, and watched.

And then, back. Troops, the music cheered,
and spoils hurried in front. Stragglers, a mile back,

hung to the final gate, faces white in the glare.
Blocking in, the Huts' shadows neared.

Inside, pinned down again, they trawled dark
nuggets from ledges, split histories.
The Davy lamp struggled in aisles. High-pitched,
they whispered, coughed, sweated salt beads.

Even a canary would die here. The thought,
regretting summer's open book, their season's
outing gone, ached for bloated skins, lax hands,
small lives measured by knuckles green as bones.

Dismissed at last, tired, they wouldn't climb,
Not without that lead. In silenced galleries,
wood, graphite, children's sweat and fear
swam in living currents, through the dust.

The Davy lamp had moved. One corner, only, shone,
flare of bindings puzzling light
with cloth. And these, their trophies,
set out on a square of hoarded chintz:

twig, feather, conker's rind, flints
foretelling axe-heads; buttercups betraying
Miss's strangled posy; all unlabelled,
muddled, with the stress of find, and leave.

– And last, cornering the corner's light,
the jagged egg, its milky base
flawed by one shallow snick:
a brittle scar of severance; a fledgling's china tear.

Snow on high ground

We shouldn't forget, in the time to come,
the time of seamless apartment block and motorway,
when the fields, ditches, marshes are already crushed
into clover-leaf and slipway, walkover, rooting underpass;

where rats stalk the old monuments, forgotten scratchings,
ringed by wire; when cattle low only in sheds;
as those above, breathing meticulously controlled air,
resort to old movies, the wall-to-wall screen, for sensation,
  views;

and we ourselves are caged, frail, bewildered by memory's
  deceptions
– still, we should not forget, nor fear to ask –
and not only by whispering in closed circles,
but in bold statement, announcement, uncategorical
  demand: Remember?

– Remember, above all else, above the unfettered rye,
and the long vistas of free rivers,
above beaches where raw cliffs sprouted, and healthy gulls
  wheeled,
above, even the vast unpeopled seas,

and the pure profiles of mountains,
their peaks unfinished by disc or aerial or funicular or café
– we should not flinch from remembering how,
in winter, when the cold clutched the bare hills,

we lived where we could see it all;
see the gnawing grey weight oppressing the fruit trees,
snared by the elders, not even shamed by the springing of
  lights

in the separate small houses; the early barking of
knowledgeable dogs;

how, shocked by the wind, the temperature's drop,
the wires' racket, we went to bed early;
woke, hours later, with a new ease, a difference;
saw the blue-black morning delivered of itself;

the sheep, awed, drawn to one side;
even the rooks silent, the light slow in coming,
as how was light needed for that quiet, aimless sparkle,
driven to the west, the gleam, although broken by turfs and
clods,

of the shy, unashamed proof? How will we forget,
or be afraid to remember, that leap in the blood,
the hills' answering look? How then, in those days,
the weather came of itself, and stayed of itself?

How once, all requirement became a simple act of faith,
so that, parting the curtains, we had only to look,
direct across the valley, and be seen, direct across the valley,
by that first, dark, arresting flush: snow on high ground?

Terra firma

Not spellable, but liked for sound, and what I thought it
meant:
the adult world, fund of fact and gesture,
the 'When I was' and 'Did you too?',
the queer creased brows, and meaning looks,
and words cut off when we were there.
Years rolling back, the Wars, the lost 'between',

and snaps to show Mum and Dad with smoother faces,
stiffer backs, outdated clothes.
They brought out mementoes, china, books of snaps,
from cupboards stuffed with things grandparents had,
meant wealth to us, who shared one teddy, scooter, trike,
shelf and a half of early books.
And mother's wardrobe, cash-box locked in furs;
baby-clothes beneath the bed;
best of all, on father's side, the upper, unlocked drawer.
'Don't,' they said 'Mustn't', which, of course,
only enlarged the thrill of checking (hoover, sink),
creeping to the sound of mother's work. Though why the
frown,
the 'No', for what was harmless, not understood?

Where sunlight came through curtains and the pines,
I dipped my wrist-bone, shuffled trove. He had so much.
But this, like strata crushed by fire and storm, was definitely
best.
Money, medals; fool's gold, I raised them, let them clatter,
rake through fingers as I lifted, turned the tins, boxes,
smells of baccy (insignia: Cut Golden Bar),
gilt cursives with jewellers' names: Edinburgh, Arbroath.
'Garnets,' Rosie said, when, once, he let us see.
'Cameos,' mother answered, touching neck and ear.
'Signet, jade, jet, locket, mourning ring,
lock of – really? – a dead person's hair?'

Also, cuff-links, châtelaine, green of brass and gold.
Who had this, who that, was forgotten, he'd pretend.
But curled certificates, student's books, a will, some
envelopes:
his name was there, quaint curly letters hard to read,
and dates, which made me pause. So very early on?

a 19, then a 12, too hard to make a sum, subtract,
find the telling difference,
though Rosie said, he must be half a century, at least.
Sometimes, pausing over a velvet ribbon, blue paste brooch,
I'd think of that; or get out his mother, Box-Brownie small,
skirts about her feet, a face like Rosie when she frowned;
or unfold the notice of death: Patrick, Daddy's daddy, 1914.

'Dead, gone, buried,' I said. But these words meant,
not so much graves, funerals, things I'd never seen;
but a wash of eras, distant, dark,
which both distinguished and secreted him:
William, Patrick's orphaned son; associate of unknown
cousins,
great-great-aunts, charmed from unreal boyhood (smock,
tartan hat),
through random studio snaps, college teams, the Home
Reserve,
embraces with grinning, leggy girls;
then one, alone, with Mummy –
the Wedding Party, with Cyril, Bertha, flowered lapels,
the beginning of the world I knew, which blossomed into
overspill;
albums, portraits stacked downstairs,
the Daddy of our family groups, with Mummy, Rosie, cat
and me.

Brought, always, back to this,
his known present shearing from his unknown past
the weight of years he'd lived without the three of us,
I knew I liked the drawer; and feared it too.
And would close it tenderly, hearing the rattle, shudder,
soft resettling of all those rich, archaic sediments,
which marked him off, made him different from me.

'Terra Firma' I used to say, of the adult world, of his.
And now death has brought us back to it,
spread over different drawers, in a different house,
seeming much thinner and plainer.
There remains only the question of who has what, and
  when;
of folding another strip of newsprint so as to link
Isobel, Patrick, Deaths Of, with their son;
of thinking how, in time, our own children will carry this
  process on,
sorting similar gimcracks of plastic and metal,
the tawdry which made us seem wealthy, secure.

They will hesitate too.
Wonder what is to be kept, what ought to be burnt.
Though nothing, not the best we can do, honours, exactly,
the way such things were treasured, and saved;
nor the personal impulse which gathered them briefly,
invested with secrets, sorrow, and love. Terra Firma?
William, who knew all the stories, and told just a few,
has gone, taking the meaning from most of these things,
now tipped onto newspaper from three shallow drawers.
Even the photos are dateless, unnamed.
And the gems all worthless – glass, nickle, and paste.

ROBERT CRAWFORD

The Dalswinton enlightenment

Patrick Miller's first iron vessel, the world's
First steamship, is swanning across Dalswinton Loch.
A landscape painter, Alexander Naysmith,
Perches on deck beside his good friend, Robert Burns.

It's a calm, clear morning. The painter will later invent
The compression rivet, and work out the axial arrangement
Between propeller and engine. The poet will write about the light
Of science dawning over Europe, remembering how

Cold sun struck Pat's boat that October day at Dalswinton
When the churning paddles articulated the loch
In triumphant metre, and the locals made some cracks,
Almost as if they were watching a ship of fools.

A Scottish assembly

Circuitry's electronic tartan, the sea,
Libraries, fields – I want the lot

To fly off and scatter, but most of all
Always to come home to roost

In this unkempt country where a handicapped printer,
Engraver of dog collars, began with his friends

The ultimate encyclopaedia.
Don't expect any rhyme or reason

For Scotland remaining an explosion reversed
Or ordinariness a fruited vine

Or why I came back here to choose my union
On the side of the ayes, remaining a part

Of this diverse assembly – Benbecula, Glasgow, Bow of
   Fife –
Voting with my feet, and this hand.

Seuils

An early morning window-cleaner tunes his radio.
Its French songs don't mist the glass. Couples

Who last night opened themselves like books
Speed up through the foreign lyrics filling

This pedestrian precinct in between
Sleeping together and office-work.

Feeling for calculators inside breast pockets
They check their keys. The days are getting longer,

Squeezing the nights. For young people in May
Glasgow is a huge anthology of prefaces.

'Let me introduce you . . .' Sunlit streets run on forever
Though everything that opens gets shut up too

Till next morning or evening – megastores, discothèques,
   foreplay –
And hovering at the back of it, mercury behind a mirror,

Are threshold demons, an old man playing a piccolo
Night after night in Nelson Mandela Place.

The Minister's marriage

Snowed-in for months with God and a model railway
That snaked round the lounge, he married a rich woman.

It was she who extended the manse
To hold more stations, a level crossing, sheds

For new locomotives, her wedding gift
Suddenly doubling the kingdom.

Through bleak midwinter in an earth-floored kitchen
The *Flying Scotsman* was never late.

One Sunday he preached a perfect sermon
About Stephenson's *Rocket*. Mostly, they did little talking.

Whenever he entered a room full of silences
He always knew which one to pick.

Dunoon

Mist becomes polythene we burst with our fingers.
Along the coastline hills are wrapped up.
Tomatoes, leeks. The country is on a level
With these things. Tugging our cold thumbs,

Petulantly pleading, love
Cannot replace shopping or the mending of telephones.
Accelerating away behind tinted windows,
The chairman drafts a long letter.

Apertures

The divorcé who photographed doors
Bored us to tears, opening up

His hobby of half a lifetime.
No two were alike: that coarse-grained barndoor in Iowa

Sagging a little, a drayman's entrance in Norfolk
Open and shut, each one with its enormous story,

Aperçus taken too far.
Then, at last, at the end of the album,

The small dark gap from which he had peeled
An apartment door that used to be his.

Kyoto

The peats stagger over the long brown cut. June
So hot that blue horses
Drift from the stained glass into the loch, Rannoch Moor
Hard as concrete. The ferry goes back and forward
Like a few simple cards reshuffled.
Crossing to the island, dragged through green water,
  crossing back.
90 in the shade. The longest day.
You could see to Kyoto
If you lent your head on my elbow.

On the way home

Che-Lan-Vien

On a clear day I abandoned the city
To go back to the mountains of the race called Hoi.

Their towers were here, gone thin with waiting,
Temples eroded under long rain.
Deserted, the river dragged in shadow. Statues
Whimpered at their open blisters.

At evening, surrounded by bending treetops,
Crowds of blind spirits linked their hands
To grope through the forest. Shadows dissolved in chaos,
Waves of scent fluttered with the sound of farewells.

Battle-sites. The souls of warriors screamed
And the blood of the Cham flowed over days.
Over months of angry injustice. Cham bones
Do not stop rustling. But there was peace once.

In the country of Chiem, yellow hamlets
Coloured by afternoon, young girls
Gone back to their village in rose-coloured dresses
That billowed over speech and laughter.

Palaces glinted in sunlight under
An open sky, a boat lay dreaming
On the still river, and beside that tower
The sacred elephants meditated together.

Evening was milky. In a light like glass or jade
The court of Chiem gazed at ivory skins
Of Chiem girls whose dreams were the song of flutes,
Their music the sway of their bodies.

I met these things on the journey home.
Days and months pass. They will not leave me.
I cannot free myself from the sadness.
The regret for the race of Hoi.

Translated from the Vietnamese by Mai-Lan and Robert Crawford.

CHE-LAN-VIEN (b. 1920), though not of the Chiem-thanh people (also known as Hoi), took up their cause and wrote poetry about their plight, similar to that of the American Indians. At the time of his writing, Hoi architecture remained only as ruins and their descendants had retreated to live in the hills, after the conquest of their land in the South of Viet-Nam.

A saying

I'm calling you late in the evening, calling
Over hundreds of miles, you cannot hear me yet.

I'm calling you by a public name, a number;
Pushing the buttons. Roundabouts will be lit

By East Kilbride headlights, Polo Mint City they call it,
Familiarly spinning its human rings of cars.

Through the machine I hear your Glasgow accent,
Your voiceprint. I just called, to say.

Beloved

Along from Helensburgh, under the unthinkable hills
Are silos. The peninsulas' prongs
Accept sunset like a dubious blessing.

A thousand mediocre landscape painters
Have botched this low light gilding the water, its slow
Turneresque burning-away.

Birdwatchers train their priestly binoculars
Round Rosneath Point over birches and brambles.
The superpowers are aware of Glen Fruin.

Photonics

We're a new technology, a system that weds
Lasers; no electronics; no gob drops
Of glass fibre to be teased and spun; just conjugate-phasing
Turning constant signals into rings of light,
A burgh packed with brilliant marriages

Strong the way a towerblock in an earthquake zone
Rocks and quivers, floating erect
On its bed of underground gravels; we're making
  discoveries,
Simplifying, unbuckling at the waist,
Unbuttoning the two pearl buttons at your throat,

Till we lie where the Giant flung his shining Causeway
Over gaunt blue water into these small sweet hills;
We meet as clearly as two beams in a saltire
Bonded at the centre, having each
Come through all the R & D to run on light.

Rain

A motorbike breaks down near Sanna in torrential rain,
Pouring loud enough to perforate limousines, long enough
To wash us to Belize. Partick's
Fish-scaled with wetness. Drips shower from foliage,
  cobbles, tourists
From New York and Dusseldorf at the tideline
Shoes lost in bogs, soaked in potholes, clarted with glaur.

An old woman is splashed by a bus. A gash
In cloud. Indians
Arrived this week to join their families and who do not feel
Scottish one inch push onwards into a drizzle
That gets heavy and vertical. Golf umbrellas
Come up like orchids on fast-forward film; exotic
Cagoules fluoresce nowhere, speckling a hillside, and
plump
Off dykes and gutters, overflowing
Ditches, a granary of water drenches the shoulders
Of Goatfell and Schiehallion. Maps under perspex go
bleary,
Spectacles clog, Strathclyde, Tayside, Dundee
Catch it, fingers spilling with water, oil-stained
As it comes down in sheets, blows
Where there are no trees, snow-wet, without thought of the
morrow.
Weddings, prunes, abattoirs, strippers, Glen Nevis, snails
Blur in its democracy, down your back, on your breasts.
In Kilmarnock a child walks naked. A woman laughs.
In cars, in Tiree bedrooms, in caravans and tenements,
Couples sleeved in love, the gibbous Govan rain.

The approach

Floating floating. In the tall dairy
Of the floods beyond, ruled with a grid of days,
Pigeons call. You remain like honey
Approaching through the hinterland, with deer abrupt
In front of the headlamps. You can absorb
Long novels of sleep and thermocouples
As the waves crash in. Night lowers its landing gear
And turns on one side. Over the telephone

Yesterday may be recounted.
Evening brindles, waiting outside the church
Pine-smells blend with the scent of cooked food.
What time is it? Like oystercatchers, breath
On the flutehole quickens us, makes us persist;
It is approaching in boatsongs, it is approaching
With loyalty running in new shoes
Through a soaking meadow, pollen-drift
Sloughed off on your bare knees.
Each of us has the laser on the disc's rotation
Dispensing arias, zither's, moon-shaped lute's.
Feathered with a tang of salt, it approaches
Floating, about to be:
Ours, when the time is proper, silent
At the sea's edge, and the surf breeze brings you
Laughing ashore from the Gulf Stream at Machrihanish.

Experiments

Engineers are munching toadfruit
With Ovid Surprize. A duck barks. It's lunch.
'I hear he put her hand right into her jeans.'
'They went from the typing pool into the bank.'

Peaceful. Only the mewing of cattle
On an idyllic English Wednesday.
But the horse weeps, lying under the coffee-table;
'They hate me because I am human.'

Mr and Mrs William Mulock in the Museum of Ethnology

Mr Mulock, staring at
The gaps between the hieroglyphs,
Shuffles his feet, and wonders what
His wife sees in that row of stiffs

Embalmed in old stone coffins. She
Is rapturous, 'The guide book said
"All visitors must go and see
The fertile Nile's immortal dead"

And now we have.' The husband coughs
But smiles to please his cultured wife;
Lost in the Pharaohs' autographs,
She disregards a common life.

Woman and man, each stands and seems
Odd, undeciphered, quite alone,
Surrounded by elusive dreams,
Fragments of the Rosetta Stone.

Inner Glasgow

You were a small red coat among the pit bings
That aren't there now, between Cambuslang
And Shettleston, with *Tell Me Why, Look and Learn*;

The quays have altered, liners replaced by jasmine;
Where docks are cultivated, hard nostalgia
Steam-rivets us to ghosts we love, in murals

Where everybody looks the same and sings
Of oppression, smokes, drinks lager, shouts out 'fuck!'
Shops sell us. Entrepreneurs' industrial

Museums postcard grime; we're pseudo-Griersonned.
But you refuse these foisted images, stay
Too true, still here, grown up in your red coat.

My inner Glasgow, you don't leave me, I
Do not leave you. A tubular steel frontage, road-cones
Flash towards us like the tiny folded pictures

In pop-up books, the lovely, lovely details
Too close to label art, that bring on laughter
When words cut out their starter motor, leaving us

Idling beside a cloudless firth. Those shorelights
Spread beyond Millport, beckon us to marry,
To lie along the bowsprits of our lives.

Scotland in the 1890s

'I came across these facts which, mixed with others . . .'
Thinking of Helensburgh, J. G. Frazer
Revises flayings and human sacrifice;
Abo of the Celtic Twilight, St Andrew Lang
Posts him a ten-page note on totemism
And a coloured fairy book – an Oxford man
From Selkirk, he translates Homer in his sleep.

'When you've lived here, even for a short time,
Samoa's a bit like Scotland – there's the sea . . .
Back in Auld Reekie with a pen that sputtered
I wrote my ballad, "Ticonderoga" or
"A Legend of the West Highlands", then returned
To King Kalakaua's beach and torches –
You know my grandfather lit Lismore's south end?'

Mr Carnegie has bought Skibo Castle.
His Union Jack's sewn to the stars and stripes.
James Murray combs the dialect from his beard
And files slips for his massive *Dictionary*.
Closing a fine biography of mother,
Remembering Dumfries, and liking boys,
James Barrie, caught in pregnant London silence,
Begins to conceive the Never Never Land.

Henry Bell introduces Europe's first commercial steamship

Scanning the universe from Helensburgh
You saw the *Comet* first in your own mind
Remote as Egypt, till it crossed the Firth
Blazing a tail of foam and smoke that seemed

Suddenly normal, the future telescoped
From the other shore. Your Cleopatran dream,
Democratised by Watt's technology
Of fire and air, burned on the water and

Made your name History. Not caring about that
A Glasgow girl at the rail, accompanied by
Two sets of radial paddles, whistled to her man
Choruses from Allan Ramsay's *The Ever Green*.

SARAH MAGUIRE

May Day, 1986
for Tadeusz Sławek

Yesterday, the weather in Warsaw
was the same as London's: 'sunny; 18°'
(sixty-four Fahrenheit). I am sitting
in a walled garden drinking gin,
the fading sky as blue as this tonic water
loosening its bubbles against the flat ice.

What is in the air? The first midges;
a television three doors down, its hum
like this lone bat avoiding the walnut tree.
A dog barks. In other houses lights come on –
the street an Advent Calendar opening
its doors. This house is in darkness,

its seven windows admitting the night.
I'm trying to read *Mansfield Park*, to learn
how Fanny finds love and a mansion
through keeping silence. All week
the weather report has plotted the wind
leaving Chernobyl with its freight

of fall-out: cancer settling on Poland –
the radioactivity an inaudible fizz
in the cells, rupturing thorax or liver,
the intimacy of the bowel. They say it won't
reach here. I stare at the sky till all
I can see are the dead cells of my eyes,

jumping and falling. It's too dark to read –
only the flare of a late *Kerria japonica*,
trained to the wall. I think of your letter
in my drawer with the handkerchiefs,
one page torn by an earlier reader. Socrates
distrusted writing, its distance from

the grain of the voice. I come indoors
to write you all the things I couldn't say
a year ago. Later, on the news, they will show
gallons of contaminated Polish milk
swilled into sewage, a boy crying
at the sting of iodine he must swallow

against the uncertain air.

Or a line of lemon sherbet

The edge of Tunisia is like the sea-side
or an abandoned set from *Beau Geste*.
It is one hundred and ten degrees.
You eat pilchards on Ryvita
and long for a sorbet
or the beginnings
of a pier.

By the time you reach the Tademait Plateau
all the hairs of your body are bleached
to the last shade of straw. Here even
your shit is a landmark. Heat bends
the horizon of ochre and orange
under a muscular sky.

Near Tamanrasset you find a spring of fresh
fizzy water. Plunging your arms into
this cold spawn you feel its gases
tick along your wrists.

The Hoggar Mountains whiten your map, their lavas
stunned into bosses and sills gothic and
measureless, cathedrals without relics
or candlesticks. You cup your palm
round an elbow of basalt and
listen to stillness.

Then you meet a hermit carrying a gas-cylinder.
For thirty years he has lived where no one
has lived, among lava and stars. His
plastic sandals are beginning
to give at the heel.

Pause in the *feche-feche* and you drown.
On your right is a blue *deux-chevaux*
up to its knees. Then the emptied
suitcase and one sling-back shoe
losing its grip.

Each night you sleep out under a big sky
and watch the North Star slip out of
reach. You envy the confident moon
intent upon leaving.

At three o'clock the night loosens its stars like
spilt salt. How you long for one to lighten
your tongue like a line of lemon sherbet
or a eucharist you could take and tuck
behind your teeth.

Eighty miles from Agadez you unscrew the last can
of spring water. You hear the dim hiss of
one thousand miles north. Small bubbles
freckle your mouth.

Spilt milk

Two soluble aspirins spore in this glass, their mycelia
fruiting the water, which I twist into milkiness.
The whole world seems to slide into the drain by my
  window.

It has rained and rained since you left, the streets black
and muscled with water. Out of pain and exhaustion you
  came
into my mouth, covering my tongue with your good and
  bitter milk.

Now I find you have cashed that cheque. I imagine you
slipping the paper under steel and glass. I sit here in a circle
of lamplight, studying women of nine hundred years past.

My hand moves into darkness as I write 'The adulterous
  woman
lost her nose and ears; the man was fined'. I drain the glass.
I still want to return to that hotel room by the station

to hear all night the goods trains coming and leaving.

The Divorce Referendum

Here, it's a fortnight to Carnival.
On hot nights I lie outside the sheets, listening to
the steel-bands practising till dawn – the throats

of oil-drums beaten to chromatics, glistening in the dark.
When it rains the railway seems to move
up the street – train after train slipping westwards

from Paddington, thickening the night.
You left from platform three. I leaned over the barrier,
my hands pressed together as if in prayer.

When you rang I was still wet from the bath. After ten years
silence you realise how you love me. I touch you
and a vessel in your feminine nose gives way –

blood and your salt-sweet tears flood my fingers and lips.
Later, my own blood inscribes the fresh sheets –
the scarlet letter, a map of desire nothing can shift.

In three months you'll leave Dublin. You tell me
the Divorce Referendum has made you choose exile.
In Camden Town you weigh a pint of Guinness in your
  palm,

drain it, push away the glass. I trace the rings
of beer-stains on the table with my finger,
or smoke your cigarettes right down to the stub.

Somewhere between here and Dún Laoghaire the boat
  broke down.
For hours you drift in the eye of your storm.
Leaning from a railing into stillness

you watch the mustard light of the ferry spill into the night,
your eyes stinging from their search for a harbour.
Later you will write, 'Perhaps I am still at sea.'

On the 'phone your voice is sallow with exhaustion,
its timbre frayed by a line carried miles under water.
When your daughter calls out in her sleep you must leave

to comfort her. I'll lie here now till dawn, twisting
the 'phone cord round my fingers till my nails turn white,
longing for suffrage, for your casting vote.

A family holiday

Most of all he hated the Irish – Papists the lot of them;
my grandfather spat in the grate. My father was in the
   scullery
trying to whistle, or fingering the willow-pattern cups.
He hung a tea-towel to dry on the back of a chair
and tapped the barometer.

'You must eat your grandad's food', my mother hissed.
In the cut-glass bowl the raspberries moved – maggots.
I covered them with a fist of sugar, watched it
haemorrhage to a juice thick as the tears of martyrs.
The cream, a blent river, turned pink.

My father and I waited in the graveyard. We could hear
my mother singing hymns slightly off-key, my grandfather
pressing the organ. My father sighed then spread *The
   Universe*
across a Methodist grave. His bottle of Guinness
left 'O's by a photograph of the Pope.

That night my window banged and split with the rain.
The sky was mustard, then alight. I counted three elephants
between the lightning and the crash. A group of children
ran in jerks beside the river; struck by lightning, one
became a Catherine wheel, staggered and went out.

'I'll take her for a walk to the farm.' My father leaned
over the gate and waved till he was small. My grandfather
said
I must help him empty the mole-traps. He tossed one at me.
Its neck was floppy and one eye had burst. I took its hand
in mine – pink, smaller than a doll's.

Freud in Paris 1885–6

'To Charcot must be ascribed the most important influence
in turning Freud from a neurologist into a psychopathologist'
Ernest Jones

1: *The Neurologist Dreams*
Paris is frozen.
I live in a laboratory
walled with foetuses –
split buds of desire
pickled in glass.
Ebony and gaslight.
Moisture in rills
greases the dull windows.
And my tongue
in a bottle, floating.
I am one eye
condensed to a lens.
I lust for ganglia

for the medulla oblongata –
a tissue of tissues
unfolding. Accept
my slow knife.
Grant me annihilation
in the textures of velum.

2: *Charcot Mesmerises*
Mecca.

God in his frock-coat
unleashes the daemons.

The clockwork limbs –
an ecstasy of grace.

The numb skin
made palpable as fresh silk.

Tongues, pliant for wafers,
sing in six octaves

out of clacked wood.
each wreck finds her storm's eye:

'Beach with me. Come.
A huge, mesmeric harbour

beckons, beckons in the candle
and the pocket watch.'

3: *The Hysteric Dances*
'I have no legs, Professor.'

He slid three pins
into her thigh. Miraculous.

Silver breaking through
clear skin, a fresh wax –

yet female with its blond down,
its neat stipples of pores.

He turned to smile at us. 'Gentlemen –'
Then taken in his warm prayer,

his lulling, ticking nipple,
he bade her dance for us –

a pirouette of sinew and ankle
– till he clapped

and woke her into leglessness.

4: *The Psychopathologist Writes Home*
February. The city's filth refracts the spring.
The houses of the rich turn into themselves,
Jealous of warmth, of their light spilt onto the snow.
Curtains and doors are slammed shut as I pass.
I am so homesick I could kneel down and weep here,
Loosening my tears into this kind snow –
Yet I am a man, a doctor – your future husband –
I have my new silk hat and gloves to think of.
How I hunger for the smallest comfort – to come home
Late at night to find you sleeping by our fire,
Your book slipped out of grasp, open on the floor.
Alone, I seek companionship in nerves and veins,
Dissecting desires and memories unfleshed.
(Martha, the medulla has been your only rival.)
But this Charcot is a genius – he mesmerises
Chaos, draws law and method out of folly –
Hysteria is mathematical! Soon science shall reduce

The twists of Goethe to a sum. I write this to you
From my desolate room. Above the roofs of distant homes
The dawn breaks and the small stars climb.

Bed and breakfast

We have booked into a hotel room so hot
it is another cliché. We lie exhumed on this great bed,
a wedding present to an ugliest daughter.
A yellow street light shows the grain of your skin,
the small hairs puckered round your nipples.
The couple in the next room are in love.
Our tooth-glass chink-chinks on its stand in sympathy.

Fin

1
The last cigarette.
        My own blood, hissing,
becomes rain at the windows.
        In a back room
a telephone rings, unanswered.

2
Shark. Six-foot confounding the marble,
        gristle pointing the split neck.
By noon it had gone into steaks.
        The market fructified melons and mangoes.
Mange-tout.

Later, one crate of snapper.
'I wouldn't bother with those, love,' he said,
'they're all bone.'

Tactics

Soho is finished. You walk past a drunk
In a doorway sleeping with six plastic bags.
He wears one orange sock and no shoes.
So you take the last tube and then walk.
Silence and the perfume of engines.
Somewhere a scream. Glass fractures.
Or the guttural taxis absorbed with leaving.
Then silence. All night. Once you heard
A child cry out in her sleep.
You wake to a typewriter uncovered.
Light freezing the windows.
Like coming home to a dictated burglary.
Plants closed into themselves as before.
The carpet untouched. What is lost?
An address book? That sheaf of papers
You whispered to yesterday?
And you search but the place is unfingered.
Some hour with no name. The fridge
Fallen silent. You waste in this
Permafrost kitchen. So white your teeth ache.
No redemption. No cigarettes either.
Soon will come buses. Sanity as big as
Elephants.

Skip

Fridges sprout
on street corners,
a cubic fungus.

You plunder their magnets,
pod them from slit plastic
into my hands.

Like your shy gifts
of coat-hangers,
the cut-offs from carpets,

or three stumps of marble:
a fractured table-top
became a frieze of ochre and rose –

you propped the sierra
against my door. Later
I opened my toe on it

and I watched you take
the wound in your mouth.
Grateful.

Psoriasis

At five-and-a-half the skin on my knees
turned to paper and flaked off.
I would peel off the scales
and lay them on the windowsill –
each a milky carapace stippled with pores.

It was still light. I could hear
the older children hiding and
finding each other again.
I put all my toys in the bed
and slept on the floor.

No one went out now.
My father's hip-bone was crumbling away.
They had taken him to the hospital
and opened it up like an egg;
at its core was an abscess
the doctor plucked out.
One afternoon I watched him asleep,
his hands gathering the eiderdown.

My mother was frightened.
'I get on a bus and I just can't breathe.'
When I broke the tea-cup she locked
herself in the bathroom for hours.
I squeezed under my bed
and traced its paisley mattress
with my finger – the swirls and flowers
fell into themselves, repeating and
repeating into the dark.
I wondered where the pattern began.

MARK FORD

Passion play

Can we hear you, Bury? Noooeoooe!
Your tide is out
And drift-wood fires our cause.
We chip the keeper, and ram the ball home.

Our bicycle has been stolen. Thieves
Came in the night and took it;
Now I'm tanked up, and celebrating:
We chip the keeper, and ram the ball home.

To be sleepless on a starless night
In Croydon, begets a sound defence,
And vicious attack. Why lie? you wearily inquire.
We chip the keeper, and ram the ball home.

Christmas

I very much enjoyed your latest book I lied having
NOT read it. Hurrah! We're all of us bright as chickens
As if Jack liked Chrissie and Chrissie liked Jack.
Ah, we had a good season, then, we drew all five fixtures!
For Christmas, I asked my mother to knit me a tie
To go with my tunic. No! she snapped,
Go out and buy one. So off I samba –
When it was Sunday and all the shops were shut –
The streets are full enough though and there are

Some fine ankles showing through – my fertile
  imagination! –
I see mini-skirts where others see only galoshes,
I can count all my exes at the bus stop
All over with tinsel, polluting the atmosphere with
Their dirty breaths. It is lunch-time
So I hail a friend munching a pastrami sandwich –
He spotted me and then he lay flat in the snow.
'Stop playing hookey,' I yelled, 'You're grown up now!'
Then I thought – but what if something is really wrong?
I screeched to a halt beside his head
The snow spooning up into my sandals, and I shouted
'Get up, Jake,' and I toed him. Any moment
I expect him to grab me playfully by the ankle,
I quite liked the idea of a tussle in the Christmas snow
On Main St. He didn't budge though.
Only the yellow stains of the mustard from his sandwich
  drooled,
Scenting the crisp air. 'Ah, come on Jake,
You think this a rodeo?' I whisper to him,
'Why not get up?' And I threaten him with
The police, arrest, his sister in tears on the phone.
And I poured hot coffee down his throat, murmuring
'But it's the season of Goodwill, no one plays for keeps
Over Christmas.' What kept him down there,
Face in the slush, people must've seen him eating
Pastrami sandwiches before?
                                        Apparently not. I waited
All afternoon by him, chain-smoking his Camels,
And then I watched his feet disappear into the ambulance
That arrived after dark. I stamped his damp sandwich
Back into the snow. People, I thought,
Will find this when the thaw sets in

And wonder about it, shopping or on their way to work,
Birds like sparrows will nibble the sesame seeds
And wish it were Pumpernickel,
It will liven up their Easter.

Land-locked

See, no hands! she cried,
Sailing down the turnpike,
And flapped her arms like a pigeon,
And from the backseat Solomon, her spaniel, answered her
By woofing ever more madly at each passing car!
What a trek it was out west
And back again! Weeks on end she spent
Stranded in the worst motels, poor thing,
Could never quite make up her mind to go on
To go back, to stay absolutely where she was.
Such awful doubts assailed her in the prairie states –
For days she chewed her favourite gum on the hard shoulder
And whispered her difficult secrets to the wheat
Where game Solomon yelped, and, true to form,
The unmiraculous wheat only rustled through its rosary
   once more.
She sent me a postcard from somewhere
In Missouri, and then again from Amarillo,
Texas. She said she thought she'd make it
All the way to sunshine California, but she said
She couldn't promise she'd like it when she did
Or even that she'd get all the way over to the ocean there,
Which didn't surprise me or disappoint me one little bit,
And I sent one back to an address in Vegas saying,
Well why should you, unless of course you want to?

My shoulder-length hair

It can usually be done
with a telephone call
or other evidence, within the slow
drip of time, or even when
it's threatening to burst its banks!
The testy voice will recall
its mother, such and such dream sequences,
long love prayers, and their mannerisms –
and awkwardnesses – Touché.
a-e-i-o-u – oh the lost art of
being tuneful . . . the microphone
stutters, respecting the paintwork,
and the unhung curtains, and general
disorder, and the angry young
mattress nailed to the floor.

Sneaker dot-to-dot

excitement, with the bit of a bore and I each glimpsing each
other's purely imaginative vegetation,
that is, with our own two eye-pieces, up and down, there
being no way out of here while the night watch
grins and stares so. At last we lay beneath dowdy green
skies, then off
to be touched by some arch-fiend's idea of a typical, well-
equipped extravaganza, high broody clouds in the
distance,
but too airy, too like collapse.

relaxing, with extra-hard idleness, dimmed night-shades,
rare phosphor

explosions, and the raw earth lapping the corrugated walls of
the hut. Just
hark at the nightjar, consider the machine-worker, search for
corrosion. Rat-
a-tat-tat small fire clashes with the boom of heavy artillery, I
take out my
gleaming silver sword, my grandfather's, and polish it.

sleep, the fire crackles according to its own sweet will. Why
feed it? For
the sake of the dry life, sweet temperance for ever! Red
swing doors open on the empty
cabaret and reveal my singer and her duck-backed manager.
It's she who with firm dislike sinks
lifeless in my arms each night, until I console her – with the
news, with money, and with the wild stories
with which I interpret her dreams.

A head for heights

Therefore a host of madmen
Have grown to love this sunny spot
And the expansive view of the city it affords.
While I clatter shut the lid of our faded
Lunch-box, you shelter your eyes from the dazzling horizon
That surrounds us, sprinkled with trees
And speeding towards us and the magnificent city spread out
For us, like a map, on the brown, bumpy plain at our feet.

But where do they come from
These early voyagers of spring, hushed
And stricken and camouflaged among the waving trees?
No one knows. And the gathering roar of exploding leaves
Behind them, in contrast, the sap
And hidden movements, brand us
Conclusively, I think; the rustling forest
Must provide fruit, and quiet pools for bathing.
But leaving aside this, how awkwardly you move,
My dear, forgetting my companion must be spryer
Than any monkey, with limbs immaculate, and a walker
Of great distances, and that day and night
You must continually seek to astonish me
With your vital gift for life.

In the Adirondacks

Bumbling with a jackass haircut through the stormy weather
With my two companions, both fresh and witty – after a while
We were introduced, formally, and after that I enticed them on
With promises of extra time. Our two bloods fought,
The bloods of moraine and of ether, admiring the prospect
Exactly where the heavy snow covered the peaks and valleys, and lay waiting
For my perspiring friends to relax, and call for a new enterprise, a halt, an explanation,

Or indeed for me to kick their stubborn behinds . . .
I thought – like a thorn – here is my weary foot thudding
through
Their winter padding, its neat quilts and roughened oil-
skins,
Fierce with exhaustion and contempt! I ripped
The gaudy strings of pearls from around their necks.
I derived no pleasure from stripping their mounted layers of
clothing
Nor from exposing their healthy bodies to the wind.
Now, as I write, with my own pen, wifeless, rich and
comfortable,
With how little pleasure do I recall that disastrous vacation
in the Adirondacks.

Cross-section

We all knew of his exploits –
The flowers from the dean's wife for his overhead,
The chair carved into an oak tree bearing his name,
And the day he passed his driving test
Wine in hall for all.
A songster
Left out in the rain trills bleakly
It's morning: new habits for me too,
Sawing things palely in half on my saw-horse
Each Sunday afternoon.

I'm

I'm an aggressive man
Always walking up escalators
And sniffing out rights. Sharks
Infest our local waters,
You too I despise.
                    Night floods the land.
We must leave now. Armies of flowers
Advance, stealing the oxygen
Right out of our mouths.

Course adjustment

Language *is* life (God help us)
it's more like a vinegar eye-bath to me.
Another semester. CJ and the committee
are at each other's throats again. It takes him a week
to unclench his fist after each session.
I can't help adding my penny's worth.
What does the doc say? The doc's out fishing
and advises you to join him. Picture it,
out there, in the icy stream, the water just
creeping over your waders – go ahead,
it's yours for the asking – whatever you catch
you get to eat. 'Nature's lightning's been known
to strike even her firmest favourites once,' I end up warning
   him,
but it's the bull-headed people who always
get their own way. Oklahoma was struck clean
from the curriculum. All the core courses

were overhauled, now I drum my fingers
on the lectern airily, but
with a huge frog croaking in my throat.

Resting up

Every high-rise has a special feel to it.
My window opens out onto some of the few
Miserable mean tear-aways still left to sweat
The length of this big dipper,
But for me, no. In summer
I like to lie unbuttoned on my bed, and to
The tune of distant traffic I begin to scan
Page after page of any book I chance upon
In search of the shape of certain favourite words.
Nothing happens when I find them,
Maybe my lucky stars loosen up a little,
But it's hard to tell their shifted constellations
From the gentle flap of curtains in the cooling breeze.
I'll check for footprints in the sweet powdery dust
Banked along the window-sill, and sprinkle bird-lime on the
  ledge outside,
Then evening falls – maybe I'll wake up one day
Covered in white fluff, and with a fat pigeon nesting on my
  feet!
'Lie back and think of anything'
I tell myself on these occasions, to relax my mind,
I need so much food, so much sleep, just so much sun
And exercise, to firm me up and improve my touch.

Then she said she had to go

The drawing-room was full.	The commuters half-turned
At last the angry hostess	to wave good-bye to
approached and	their friends. About their
whispered	feet fell the
black	words
into my	of their
unsuspecting ear.	evening newspapers.
My new cow	Lunch is a strange experience here.
is loose in the field.	The big hall is
With her tail she	full of birds
swishes	swooping around –
away	flies
and wanders	a carrot I
off happily to the fence.	was about to eat.
A large sea swell	The desk was littered
swamped the bay;	with books. She banged
the streets were	the front door, and I tried
drenched, and	to imagine
salt	water
was found as	flowing
far inland as Newton.	from her lovely eyes.

Chattering teeth

My teeth may chatter
But how I love her.
On frosty nights her silhouette
Dances against the brown barn door
Mocking me for something I might have said to her
During the day.
I follow the glittering points of the moon
Caught in her eyes,
Weaving towards me where I lie in the hay
Amazed at her dark moving arms
When all else is quiet asleep,
Only she in the silence
Flinging her legs in random cartwheels,
I hear clearly the touch of her bare feet
In the straw, lightly pressing the wooden boards . . .

But by dawn the stars are fading, and the dray
Is restless, wanting attention.
Such weather we're having, it won't last,
I remark outloud to myself, shivering, and watching
The sky, and imagining snow
Descending from it like a blanket,
Drift upon drift, piling up
Like a dome, around the various doors,
The roof, the attic window . . .

A swimming-pool full of peanuts

A stifling blanket day out west I was working the desert
states
nothing for days thank-you ma'am door slams in my face
(again)
so I mosey out round the back where my vehicle sits melting
I'll
just check the set-up the outhouses the grass is all stiff
and plastic the trees are all lifeless and there's no shade
nothing stirring until I come across right in the open
a whole swimming-pool full of peanuts I think
I've gone mad so I shut my eyes and I count
to five and look again and they're still resting there
very quietly an inch or so I suppose below
the high-water mark they're a light tan colour
and the tiles around are a lovely cool aqua blue
only there's no water just these peanuts.
Well this is a hoax I can tell some monkey's idea
of a good joke for who'd fill up a fair-sized swimming-
pool entirely with peanuts unless they're painted in
which case it's a nice piece of work so I
kneel down in my best suit on the edge
(tie at half-mast because of the heat)
and with a loud snigger I dip in my finger
just to see it sinks into small grainy nuggets
sand-coated and a bit greasy some whole some in
half I draw it out and examine it all shiny with oil
the nail gleaming and I lick it to find out the taste
SALT! madness! the genuine article! straight salted
peanuts!
this gets me because what kind of mad case goes
to the trouble of building a swimming-pool and then fills it

instead of with water with salted peanuts right up to the brim
I'm the butt of his jest this goop is taking the michael
almost physically I can feel him pulling my leg so
I lean over again and lower my head carefully until my
left eye is level with the glistening expanse for no
reason I'm feeling all queasy this pool full of peanuts
is disturbing my eye won't focus in case in an instant
they turn into piranha fish and green mambas
or anything else that might be hiding down there.

Still nothing moved I admit it was quiet too quiet
all I could hear was my own labouring breath
so in both clammy hands I scoop up fist after fistful
and I watch them trickle through my fingers and glitter in
the sun I go back to my car and open up the trunk
I take out my golf-bag I select a nine-iron
and without a thought for my own safety I head back
to the pool and I swing away reckless in that peanut bunker
I scatter peanuts like a madman all over around there
they go flying like sand-flies in all directions like golf-
balls they arc away and shower down like buff-coloured hail
and I thresh and flail like one possessed
but nothing is uncovered it's no good from the edge
so feet first I leap in at the deep end
brandishing my golf-club and hit away
like a good soldier but there's more and more always
though I swing a good hour at the end of that
I am exhausted and my skin itches from the salt
and my clothes are all clinging I collapse in the middle
buoyed up by the peanuts the whole thing is hopeless
my pores are all clogged so I say let sleeping dogs lie
and I crawl to the side and haul myself out and
shake out the loose peanuts from the creases of my suit

I pick them out of my socks and empty out my shoes
I brush them out of my armpits and angrily I throw
my nine-iron into the middle of the pool where it sinks
without trace and I storm back to my car and
I make this resolution never ever if you can ever avoid it
fool around with a swimming-pool like this one
well a swimming-pool of peanuts is not worth the trouble.

Outing

Ever since a willing spirit took me up
and began work on my reflexes, it feels
like I'm living the life my ancestors lived, though
I always imagine them as a wealthy jungle-dwelling people,
forever under the dripping elms.
If only it were truly impossible, and less like being a huge
  green amphibian
made to inch my home-sick coils between the different
  counters
of your favourite store, taking all these fancy cautions
to keep my head down, and out of other shoppers' way.
Your ankles I can just make out. The cash till rings,
though I'll never know what you at last decided on
out of so vast a choice of things, quite naturally
you refused to wait until the crush thinned out.
The dusty floor is cool, like a fountain,
worn smooth and comfortable by so many feet.
The trusty bell-boy follows obediently in your wake . . .
Now as I glide towards the whirr of sliding doors, I half-
  hope

its electric eye won't respond to my irregular approach.
   Another
spanking clean threshold! 'Open Sesame,' it cries, 'Hold
   tight!',
in its familiar Southern drawl, 'You know me well,
I won't be going to go to Hell for anybody.'

BIOGRAPHICAL NOTES

SUSANNE EHRHARDT was born in Germany in 1944 and grew up there. She read Chinese at the School of Oriental and African Studies, London, and later qualified in Medicine from the University of Cambridge. She has lived in Bangladesh for about six years and now lives and works in England. Three of the poems included here first appeared in the *London Review of Books*, under the name of Chowdhury. The poem 'Footnotes to the Tour Report' was previously published as 'Disaster Area'.

PAUL MAY was born in Aberdeen in 1963. He read English at Lady Margaret Hall, Oxford and began writing poetry in 1984. His other writings include a first play which was performed on the Edinburgh Fringe in 1985. He currently works for a national educational organisation and lives in North London.

Several of the poems in this selection were first printed in the *New Statesman*.

LUCY ANNE WATT was born in 1951 and educated at the Universities of Nottingham and Manchester. She took a postgraduate teacher-training course outside Oxford, and an intensive secretarial course at Pitman's Central College. She has worked as a shop assistant, nanny, assistant occupational therapist with geriatrics; teacher, typist, and occasional editorial assistant on national magazines and newspapers. She has also up-dated two flats and one garden, and is now working on a Regency house and its gardens in Dorset, where she has a very small business. Her poems have appeared in *Ambit*, *Country Life*, *Grand Piano*, *The*

Green Book, *The Honest Ulsterman*, the *Literary Review*, the *London Review of Books*, *The Mandeville Bestiary*, *New Statesman*, *Other Poetry*, *Poetry Review*, *Slow Dancer*, *Writing Women*, and other publications.

ROBERT CRAWFORD was born in 1959 at Bellshill, near Glasgow. He grew up and went to school in Glasgow, and studied English at Glasgow University. In 1981 he was awarded a Carnegie Scholarship and Snell Exhibition to Balliol College, Oxford, where he wrote a doctoral thesis on T. S. Eliot, under the supervision of Richard Ellmann. Between 1984 and 1987 he was Elizabeth Wordsworth Junior Research Fellow at St Hugh's College, Oxford. The award of a three-year British Academy Postdoctoral Fellowship then allowed him to return to the Department of English Literature at Glasgow University to work on connections between Scottish culture and Modernism. In 1984, with the Scottish poet David Kinloch and the American poet Henry Hart, he started the international magazine *Verse*, still going strong under its original editors. With Dundonian W. N. Herbert and David Kinloch he also began publishing pamphlets of poetry in Scots (*Sterts & Stobies*, 1985; *Severe Burns*, 1986). In 1987 Robert Crawford was a runner-up in the National Poetry Competition; in 1988 he won a Gregory Award, and first prize in the McCash competition for poetry in Scots. Recent poems have appeared in *Cencrastus*, *London Magazine*, *London Review of Books*, *New Writing Scotland*, and *Verse*, as well as being broadcast on BBC Radio 3 and in Scottish Television's *In Verse* series. In 1987 he published *The Savage and the City in the Work of T. S. Eliot* (OUP). He lives in Glasgow.

SARAH MAGUIRE was born in west London in 1957, where she has continued to live, her home being in Notting Hill since 1974. After a reluctant education she left school to work as an apprentice gardener, becoming a Craftswoman Gardener after three years. Following this she worked for Release, the legal information and drugs agency. She then had a variety of part-time jobs in adult education and as a solicitor's Outdoor Clerk. In 1984 she went to the University of East Anglia to read English. She is currently researching into femininity in the eighteenth-century novel for a PhD at the University of Cambridge. Her poems have been published in the *London Review of Books*. She received a prize in the 1985 National Poetry Competition and a Special Commendation in the 1987 Arvon International Poetry Competition. She is co-editor of the journal *Poetry Now*.

MARK FORD was born in 1962. He was educated at St Paul's School, London, and at Lincoln College, Oxford. In 1983 he was awarded a Kennedy Scholarship to Harvard University. His poems have been published in the *London Review of Books*, *North Magazine*, *Oxford Poetry*, *Poetry Review*, the Bloomsbury anthology *Soho Square* and *The Times Literary Supplement*.

He is currently a lecturer at University College, London; his articles have appeared in the *Independent*, the *Literary Review*, the *London Review of Books*, *Oxford Poetry*, *The Times Literary Supplement*, and *Verse*.

He now lives in New Cross Gate, London.